Joseph's Journey

Volume 3

*A Look at the Flip Side
of My Life*

Joseph's Journey

Volume 3

*A Look at the Flip Side
of My Life*

by

Joseph Fram

Everlasting Publishing
Yakima, Washington USA

Joseph's Journey
Volume 3

A Look at the Flip Side of My Life

by
Joseph Fram

Library of Congress Control Number
2006910724

ISBN: 0-9778083-4-3
ISBN-13: 978-0-9778083-4-2

First Edition
Everlasting Publishing
P.O. Box 1061
Yakima, WA 98907

My dad, Joseph Fram, never ceases to amaze me. Ever since I was a child, I have been impressed by his intelligence and his compassion, and as I grew, I discovered that his accomplishments have been truly amazing. When I read the poems he wrote for this book, I was touched, enlightened, moved, and encouraged. I have grown closer to my dad through his poetry. I am so thankful that he's my dad, the best dad in the world.

Dana Fram Pride

Dedicated to my daughter, Dana Fram Pride, who has been instrumental in my publications, and to my son, Dale Fram, whose music inspired some of my poetry. There are dark moments in each person's life that can only be brightened by his children. Thank you, Dana and Dale, for the light at those times.

Joseph Fram

JOSEPH'S JOURNEY VOLUME 3

A LOOK AT THE FLIP SIDE OF MY LIFE

MY CHILDREN
by
Joseph Fram

THANK YOU FOR YOUR TIME
AND THE LIFE YOU LET ME SHARE
ALL THE LOVE YOU GAVE
GOT ME FROM HERE TO THERE

I NOW UNDERSTAND GOD'S PLAN
FOR HE KNOWS WHAT TO DO
HE SMOOTHED MY ROCKY ROAD
WHEN HE LET ME WALK WITH YOU

IT'S KNOWN FAMILIES HAVE TO GROW
AND NOW IT IS TIME TO PART
THOUGH MILES BE BETWEEN US
YOU ARE ALWAYS IN MY HEART

SO GODSPEED LITTLE ONES
LET LOVE GUIDE YOU FROM NOW ON
I WILL SAY MY PRAYERS TO HELP YOU
AND KEEP YOU SAFE FROM DUSK TO DAWN

IF YOU EVER NEED ME
CLOSE YOUR EYES I WILL BE THERE
BECAUSE A FATHER'S LOVE
CAN FIND YOU ANYWHERE

IMAGINE

by
Joseph Fram

IMAGINE A WORLD
IN WHICH CHRIST WOULD LIVE
A WORLD FULL OF LOVE
TO TAKE AND TO GIVE

WHERE ALL THAT SURROUND US
WERE KIND TO EACH OTHER
AND FORGIVE US OUR SINS
LIKE TRUE SISTER AND BROTHER

WHERE ALL UNKIND DEEDS
WERE DONE BY MISTAKE
AND WE WELCOME STRANGERS
AS A NEW FRIEND TO MAKE

WHERE, WHEN ONE GOT HURT
ALL WOULD COME TO THEIR AID
WITH NO THOUGHT OF PAYMENT
CAUSE WITH LOVE IT WAS PAID

IMAGINE A CHRISTMAS
THAT LASTS A LONG WHILE
THEN IMAGINE CHRIST WATCHING
AND IMAGINE HIS SMILE

A PERFECT ROSE

by
Joseph Fram

WHY RECONSTRUCT A PERFECT ROSE
EACH PETAL NEATLY IN ITS PLACE
TO TAMPER WITH A GIFT OF GOD
IS NOT FOR THE HUMAN RACE

HE HAS MADE ONE AND ALL
TO BE THE WAY THAT THEY SHOULD BE
TO CHANGE A SINGLE THING HE DOES
IS NOT FOR YOU AND NOT FOR ME

WHEN YOU ASK WHAT I WOULD CHANGE
WHAT IS THERE FOR ME TO SAY
HAD YOU NOT BEEN AS YOU ARE
I WOULDN'T BE WITH YOU TODAY

I JUST ASK THAT YOU GO BACK
AND SEE THE WAY YOU ARE
FOR HE HAS DONE A BETTER JOB
THAN I CAN DO BY FAR

PLEASE DON'T CHANGE FOR ANYONE
UNLESS IT'S IN THE MIND OF YOU
ONCE YOU CHANGE WHAT GOD HAS MADE
IS THE DAY THAT YOU ARE THROUGH

LITTLE FINGERS
by
Joseph Fram

LITTLE FINGERS WORK THE GOLD
TO MAKE IT PLEASANT TO THE EYE
AND BECAUSE IT IS SO RARE
FOR IT YOU SEE MEN DIE

GOLD AND ALL ITS BEAUTY
HAS A VALUE THAT'S WELL KNOWN
BUT IT IS ONLY METAL
WHEN IT IS LEFT ALONE

LOVE IS JUST LIKE THAT METAL
LITTLE FINGERS NEED TO MAKE THEIR MARK
FOR IT WILL JUST LIE WITHIN YOU
WITHOUT THE LITTLE FINGERS SPARK

JUST LIKE GOLD, LOVE STAYS THERE
NO MATTER WHERE IT'S PLACED
YOU CAN ALWAYS MAKE IT SHINE
IT MATTERS NOT WHAT IT HAS FACED

WHEN LOVE OR GOLDEN CHAIN IS BROKEN
LITTLE FINGERS JUST KNOW HOW
TO PUT THEM BACK TOGETHER
THEN THEY ARE JUST AS GOOD AS NOW

LOCKED IN TIME

by
Joseph Fram

EACH ACTION THAT WE TAKE
IS LOCKED IN TIME AND SPACE
IT IS THERE FOREVER
WHAT IS DONE WE CAN'T ERASE

IF WE TAKE A BACKWARD GLANCE
SOMETIMES WE WONDER WHY
BUT IT WAS DONE LOCKED IN TIME
FOR REASONS FAR BEYOND THE EYE

NOW IT MAY SEEM UNREASONABLE
BUT THAT WAS WAY BACK THEN
SO BEING LOCKED IN TIME AND SPACE
WE WOULD DO IT ALL AGAIN

OUR LIFE IS NOT A DIAGRAM
WE ACT SOME TIME IN FRIGHT
SO WHATEVER THING WE DID
AT THE TIME WE THOUGHT IT RIGHT

IT DOES NO GOOD TO SECOND GUESS
THE MIND WAS MADE BACK THEN
BASED ON WHAT YOU HAD AT HAND
LOCKED IN TIME AND NOT AGAIN

CHOIR OF ANGELS
by
Joseph Fram

I HEARD A CHOIR OF ANGELS
AS AVE MARIA FILLED THE AIR
WHEN I OPENED UP MY EYES
I SAW THAT THEY WEREN'T THERE

I WAS ALONE IN CHURCH THAT DAY
WITH BROKEN HEART AND FULL OF TEARS
JUST TO SAY A LITTLE PRAYER
IN HOPES 'TWOULD WASH AWAY MY FEARS

THE CHURCH THAT I WAS SITTING IN
BROUGHT ME COMFORT AS A BOY
AND I KNEW THAT GOD LIVED THERE
AND ONLY HE COULD BRING ME JOY

I MUST HAVE LOST TRACK OF MY TIME
FOR WHEN I LOOKED AROUND TO SEE
THE CHURCH WAS FULL OF PEOPLE
AND PRAYER SURROUNDED ME

AGAIN I HEARD THE ANGEL CHOIR
AS THE CHILDREN SANG THEIR SONG
AS PEACEFULNESS FILLED MY HEART
I KNEW IT WAS THERE THAT I BELONG

IN YOUR HEART
by
Joseph Fram

IF YOU HAVE IT IN YOUR HEART
YOU CAN DO MOST ANYTHING
MAYBE WRITE A POEM LIKE THIS
AND EVEN MAKE IT SING

JUST LOOK INSIDE YOURSELF
YOU HAVE SO MUCH TO GIVE
YOU CAN MAKE THE WORLD YOUR FRIEND
FOR AS LONG AS YOU MAY LIVE

YOU WILL HIT A BUMP OR TWO
OTHERS MAY SAY THAT YOU ARE WRONG
BUT THE THING THEY CAN'T HEAR
ARE THE WORDS IN YOUR OWN SONG

I ASK YOU NOT BETRAY YOURSELF
FROM THAT DAY YOU'LL HAVE REGRET
OH, YOU WILL STUMBLE ON THROUGH LIFE
BUT THE BETRAYAL DATE YOU'LL NOT FORGET

SO IF YOU KEEP TO YOUR HEART
YOU'LL BE HAPPY THROUGH AND THROUGH
ONLY YOU CAN BETRAY YOURSELF
DOING THINGS YOU OUGHT NOT TO DO

CHRISTMAS BLESSINGS
by
Joseph Fram

IT WAS A TIME OF CHEER
AND SLEIGH BELLS IN THE SNOW
WITH CHRISTMAS LIGHTS ON CHRISTMAS TREES
JUST LIKE THE ONES WE USED TO KNOW

IT WAS THAT TIME OF YEAR
WHEN CHILDREN LAUGH AND PLAY
AND THEIR LITTLE EYES LIGHT UP
TO SEE SANTA IN HIS SLEIGH

IT WAS THE TIME OF SCHOOL PROGRAMS
WHEN CHILDREN DREAM ALL NIGHT LONG
AND THEY PRACTICE REALLY HARD
TO SING THEIR CHRISTMAS SONG

IT WAS A TIME FOR PRESENTS
FOR ALL THE GIRLS AND BOYS
AND THE CHRISTMAS TREE WAS BEAMING
WITH EVERY KIND OF TOY

THEN IT WAS A TIME TO REMEMBER
AMID EMPTY WRAPPERS THAT MORN
THE REASON THAT THERE IS CHRISTMAS
IS THE DAY CHRIST CHILD WAS BORN

DOREEN

by
Joseph Fram

YOU TOUCHED MY HEART
IN A TENDER WAY
THE NIGHT I FEARED
BECAME THE BRIGHTEST DAY

YOUR GENTLE TOUCH
AT NIGHT'S END
TOLD MY HEART
IT HAD A FRIEND

TO TOUCH A HEART
LOST IN TIME
MAKES LIFE'S MOUNTAIN
AN EASY CLIMB

THAT TENDER SPOT
YOU LEFT THAT DAY
IN A SPECIAL PLACE
WILL FOREVER STAY

G.O.L.F

by

Joseph Fram

I HAD A STRANGE ENCOUNTER
ON A GOLF COURSE ONE FINE DAY
WHEN I CAUGHT UP WITH SOME WOMEN
POINTED OUT THEY'RE IN THE WAY

THEY REALLY GOT INDIGNANT
WHEN TO THEM I EXPLAINED THE GAME
GENTLEMEN ONLY LADIES FORBIDDEN
IS WHAT THAT STANDS FOR IN THE NAME

THEY LOOKED AMAZED AND PUZZLED
THEY HAD NOT HEARD THAT BEFORE
WHEN IT FINALLY REGISTERED
THEY CHOSE TO HEAR NO MORE

WHEN I ASKED THEY LET ME THROUGH
THEY POLITELY LET ME BY
BUT WHEN I WENT TO TEE OFF
MY LAST VISION WAS THE SKY

WHEN I AWOKE NEXT MORNING
I CURSED GOLF AND ITS NAME
FROM THE SORRY SHAPE I WOUND UP
I'D SAY MEN AND WOMEN ARE THE SAME

TO HELEN

by
Joseph Fram

WHAT A GREAT SISTER
I'VE HAD THROUGH THE YEARS
ONE WHO STOOD BY ME
THROUGH ALL TROUBLE AND FEARS

YOUR PRAYERS HAVE BEEN WELCOME
IN HAPPINESS AND DESPAIR
AND NO MATTER THE OUTCOME
YOU HAVE ALWAYS BEEN THERE

YOU KNOW THE MEANING OF FAMILY
AND WHAT TO DO WITH A STRAY
YOU KEEP TRUST IN GOD
TO MAKE IT RIGHT ONE DAY

THOUGH YOU NEVER MADE HEADLINES
FOR ALL OTHERS TO SEE
YOUR LOVE FOR YOUR FAMILY
IS JUST RIGHT FOR ME

GOD BLESS YOU FOREVER
SAINTHOOD SURELY AWAITS YOU
YOU'LL GO STRAIGHT TO HEAVEN
WHEN THIS LIFE IS THROUGH

GAMBLE
by
Joseph Fram

I HAVE ROLLED A DICE OR TWO
JUST TO TRY MY LUCK
BUT THE DEALER'S SMILE AT ME
TELLS ME I'M A SITTING DUCK

AND AT CARDS I PLAY A HAND
THEY LET ME WIN A LITTLE BIT
JUST AS I THINK I HAVE IT MADE
THEY HAVE THEIR BIGGEST HIT

I HAVE READ SO MANY BOOKS
ON HOW TO PLAY THE SLOTS
BUT MY MONEY ALL RUNS OUT
BEFORE I FIGURE OUT THE PLOTS

I USED TO PLAY THE RACES TOO
MY FAVORITE HORSE I'D BET
SOMEHOW PICKING THE NAME I LIKE
HASN'T BROUGHT ME MONEY YET

SO I HAVE GIVEN THOUGHT TO GAMBLE
IT'S NOT ALL THAT IT WOULD SEEM
IT IS DESIGNED TO MAKE YOU BROKE
WHILE IT GIVES YOU HOPE TO DREAM

GREEN BLOCKED

by
Joseph Fram

WELL, I NEVER SAW IT COMING
IT JUST HIT ME LIKE A TRAIN
WHEN YOU LEFT THAT LITTLE PACKAGE
IT WAS A BOXCAR FULL OF PAIN

AND WHEN THAT BOX WAS OPENED
PAIN JUST POURED UPON THE GROUND
I TRIED TO SCOOP UP ALL THE PIECES
BUT THEY WERE SCATTERED ALL AROUND

WHEN I OPENED UP THAT TINY BOX
NO BIGGER THAN A SAD GOODBYE
A BOXCAR COULDN'T HOLD THE TEARS
ONCE MY EYES BEGAN TO CRY

THEN THAT TRAIN BECAME SO LONG
WHEN I'D ADD A BOXCAR TO THE END
UNTIL ONE DAY I PUSHED SO HARD
IT GOT LOST AROUND THE BEND

I'M SURE GLAD THAT TRAIN IS GONE
IT'S CLEARED THE TRACKS YOU SEE
A PULLMAN CAR JUST FULL OF LOVE
IS GREEN BLOCKED JUST FOR ME

13

GROWING OLD
by
Joseph Fram

OF GROWING OLD
I HAVE HEARD A LOT
BUT NOT TOO MUCH
OF THE THINGS I'VE GOT

OH, YES I AGE
BUT I DO NOT GROW OLD
THINGS I DO ARE YOUNG
SO I'VE BEEN TOLD

AND OF THOSE THINGS
I CAN'T BRING TO MIND
ARE BEST FORGOT
MOST TIMES I FIND

IF ONE STAYED THE SAME
FOR THEIR WHOLE LIFE THROUGH
THEY COULD LEARN ONE THING
AND NOT ONE THING NEW

OF GROWING OLD
I'M NOW NOT KNOWING
INSTEAD I THINK
I JUST KEEP GROWING

SWEET DOREEN

by
Joseph Fram

SWEET DOREEN IS A PART OF ME
AS OUR YEARS TOGETHER GROW
JUST HOW TENDER IS HER LOVE
SWEET DOREEN WILL NEVER KNOW

SHE IS HAPPY WHEN I'M HAPPY
SHE IS STRONG WHEN I AM WEAK
AND IF I SHOULD EVER RAGE
SHE JUST SMILES AS I SPEAK

SWEET DOREEN HAS HAD HER TROUBLES
IT IS NOT IN HER TO COMPLAIN
SHE ENDURES THEM DEEP WITHIN
TILL SHE IS SWEET DOREEN AGAIN

IT IS NOT THAT I JUST LOVE HER
SHE REALLY IS MY BEST FRIEND
LIKE WITH SO MANY OF HER OTHERS
SHE NEVER LETS A FRIENDSHIP END

SWEET DOREEN TELLS ME SHE'S MINE
SHE MAKES ME INTO A KING
I'D WISH ALL A SWEET DOREEN
IF I COULD ONLY WISH ONE THING

HALF WAY DONE

by
Joseph Fram

THE FIRST DAY OF MY RETIREMENT
I THOUGHT I'D BE AT MY WIT'S END
I HAD WORKED ALL MY LIFE
AND WORK HAD BECOME MY FRIEND

WHEN I LEFT I LOST THAT FRIEND
I THOUGHT NO ONE COULD REPLACE
WITHOUT THE WORK I WAS ALONE
LOOKING FOR ANOTHER PACE

OH, I TRIED SOME DIFFERENT THINGS
PLAYING GOLF AND BOWLING TOO
OR WHATEVER GAME THERE WAS
I THOUGHT I STILL COULD DO

THEN ONE DAY I SET A GOAL
I KNEW I COULD ACHIEVE
TO HELP ME GREET THE DAY
AND ALL MY TENSIONS TO RELIEVE

FOR MY GOAL IS SIMPLE
EVERY DAY MY RACE IS WON
I GET UP WITH NAUGHT TO DO
AND TRY TO GET IT HALF WAY DONE

GOD'S REASON

by
Joseph Fram

EVERY SINGLE DEED WE DO
IS SET BEFORE IT'S DONE
NO MATTER HOW WE CHANGE IT
IT'S THE SAME AS WHEN BEGUN

ALL THE THINGS WE PLAN
ARE SET FORTH AS IN STONE
SOMETIMES WE DON'T REALIZE IT
IN THIS WE ARE NOT ALONE

GOD HAS REASONS OF HIS OWN
FOR ALL THAT HAPPENS IN OUR LIFE
SOMETIMES HE BRINGS US HAPPINESS
OTHER TIMES HE BRINGS US STRIFE

WE REALLY HAVE NO QUARREL
WHEN EVERYTHING GOES RIGHT
WITH LOVED ONES ALL AROUND US
AND WE GET ALL WITHOUT A FIGHT

BUT WHEN THERE IS TRAGEDY
GOD HAS A REASON FOR THAT TOO
IF YOU SEEK YOU WILL FIND IT
GOD WILL SHOW YOU WHAT TO DO

HAPPY VOLUNTEERS
by
Joseph Fram

BUSY, BUSY, BUSY
DEDICATED VOLUNTEERS TOIL
THEY NEED TO KEEP ON AGOIN'
THEIR RETIREMENT NOT TO SPOIL

THEY LOVE WHAT THEY ARE DOING
THEY HAVE WAITED FOR SO LONG
WHEN THEY SAT DOING NOTHING
THEY KNEW SOMEHOW IT FELT WRONG

IN ANOTHER LIFE
THEY DID THEIR WORK FOR PAY
BUT NOW IT IS A WORK OF LOVE
THEY'D HAVE IT NO OTHER WAY

OH, I SEE THEM BLOSSOM
AS THEY UNDERTAKE THEIR TASK
IS THERE MORE FOR DOING
I OFTEN HEAR THEM ASK

THEY LOVE THE LIFE THEY'RE LIVING
THEY HAVE WAITED ALL THEIR LIFE
TO DO THE THINGS THEY WANT TO DO
AWAY FROM TROUBLE, TOIL AND STRIFE

HEAVEN'S BOAT
by
Joseph Fram

HEAVEN'S BOAT MADE ITS EARTHLY ROUNDS
GOD CALLED GARY OUT BY NAME
ALL THE LOVE YOU LEAVE ON EARTH
IN MY HOUSE WILL BE THE SAME

THERE IS NO MORE THAT YOU CAN DO
YOU HAVE SPREAD MY WORD OF LOVE
IT WILL REMAIN WITH THOSE YOU LEFT
I'LL HELP YOU SHARE IT FROM ABOVE

YOU STAYED THE MAN I MADE OF YOU
YOU SAW ONLY GOOD IN ALL AROUND
ALL THE KINDNESS THAT YOU SHARED
REFLECTS IN ALL THE FRIENDS YOU FOUND

FOR THE WIFE YOU LEFT BEHIND
I ASK THAT YOU HAVE NO FEAR
I'VE ALSO MADE A PLACE FOR HER
WHEN IT IS TIME TO JOIN YOU HERE

SO COME WITH ME DEAR GARY
ENJOY THE PEACE YOU'LL FIND
THERE IS NO DEATH WHERE YOU GO
I'LL LEAVE YOUR MEMORY BEHIND

BLANK

by

Joseph Fram

MANY TIMES I WONDER
HOW THINGS SLIP MY MIND
WHERE I AM CERTAIN I PUT THINGS
LATER ON THAT I CAN'T FIND

LIKE A COUPLE DAYS AGO
A TREASURE I PUT SAFELY IN ITS PLACE
I KNEW I WOULD REMEMBER IT
NOW MY SEARCH IS A FRANTIC RACE

OR I WILL WALK INTO A ROOM
TO DO SOME SIMPLE TASK
NO SOONER DO I GET IN THERE
"WHY DID I COME IN HERE" I WILL ASK

THERE ARE BLANKS AND BLANKS
IN MANY THINGS I DO
WHEN I TELL THEM TO MY FRIENDS
THEY SAY "I HAVE THEM TOO"

FINALLY IT DAWNED ON ME
THAT MY MIND IS HALF WAY GONE
WHEN I SPENT A GOOD HALF HOUR
LOOKING FOR THE SHOES THAT I HAD ON

HIGHLANDS REMEMBERED

(1954–1956)

by

Joseph Fram

STUDY, STUDY, STUDY
THAT IS ALL I USED TO DO
NO TIME FOR FUN AND GAMES
A QUICK DEGREE, THEN I AM THROUGH

YES, I FINISHED QUICKLY
TWO DEGREES WERE IN MY HAND
I MUST HAVE SET SOME RECORD
FOR THIS I THOUGHT THAT I WAS GRAND

THEN CAME FAME AND FORTUNE
A HARD NOSE WORKER I BECAME
I NEVER TOOK A SICK DAY
I TURNED WORK INTO MY GAME

NOW SADLY I REMEMBER
ALL THOSE FUN TIMES THAT I MISSED
THE OTHER SIDE OF COLLEGE
THE PRETTY GIRLS I NEVER KISSED

IF ONLY I HAD KNOWN THEN
COLLEGE IS MADE TO MAKE YOU GROW
IN SOCIAL SKILLS AND FRIENDSHIPS
NOT ONLY THINGS TO KNOW

HOW TO LOVE ME
by
Joseph Fram

HOW DID YOU KNOW HOW TO LOVE ME
HOW DID YOU GET INTO MY MIND
HOW DID YOU KNOW YOU'D LOSE ME
UNLESS YOU WERE GENTLE, SWEET AND KIND

I HAD BEEN WITH OTHERS
WITH THEM I DIDN'T STAY TOO LONG
YES, THEY HAD THEIR CHARMS ABOUT THEM
BUT TO ME IT FELT SO WRONG

THEY HAD LOOKED AT ME FROM OUTSIDE
THOUGHT I WAS STRONG AS CAN BE
SOMEHOW YOU LOOKED BEYOND THAT
TO A WEAK HEART BEAT WITHIN ME

HOW DID YOU KNOW I LOVE YOUR TOUCH
AND THE WARMTH OF YOUR KISS GOODNIGHT
AND WHEN I WAS LOST AND LONELY
YOUR TENDER ARMS COULD HOLD ME TIGHT

I DIDN'T LOOK FOR LOVE THAT DAY
NOR THINK IT COULD BE FOUND
BECAUSE YOU KNEW HOW TO LOVE ME
I'M NO LONGER HELL WARD BOUND

CHRISTMAS IN HEAVEN

by
Joseph Fram

SINCE CHRISTMAS LAST
LOVED ONES HAVE DIED
THERE IS PAUSE TO PONDER
AFTER I HAVE CRIED

IS THERE CHRISTMAS IN HEAVEN
DOES GOD PUT UP A TREE
FOR ALL OF HIS CHILDREN
LIKE MY FOLKS DID FOR ME

WHAT KIND OF PRESENTS
AND HOW ARE THEY BOUND
ARE THERE CHRISTMAS SURPRISES
AFTER THEY'RE FOUND

THE KIND OF CHRISTMAS IN HEAVEN
I HAVE IN MY MIND
IS EVERLASTING HAPPINESS
IN ONLY HEAVEN YOU'LL FIND

IT IS GOOD TO REMEMBER
AT CHRISTMAS THOSE THAT WE LOVE
SPENDING CHRISTMAS IN HEAVEN
AND WATCHING US FROM ABOVE

I RECKON

by

Joseph Fram

I RECKON I'VE DONE SOME GOOD
PROBABLY DONE SOME BAD
FEEL HAPPY ABOUT THE GOOD
THE OTHER MAKES ME SAD

GUESS I MAY HAVE HURT SOME
BUT I MAY HAVE HELPED SOME TOO
HOPE THE ONES I HELPED ARE MANY
AND THE ONES I HURT ARE FEW

IT'S KINDA HARD TO KNOW
WHAT YOU DO IS WRONG OR RIGHT
I DON'T DO THINGS TO HURT ONES
THOUGH SOMETIMES THEY JUST MIGHT

I CAN'T KNOW ANOTHER'S FEELINGS
OR RECKON HOW THEY TOOK WHAT'S DONE
I NEVER KNOW IF THEY TOOK SERIOUS
SOMETHING I MIGHT HAVE DONE IN FUN

I RECKON IN THE GAME OF LIFE
IT IS HARD TO CORRECT THE WRONG
I RECKON THE BEST WE HOPE FOR
GIVEN HURT WON'T LAST TOO LONG

PARADISE IN MY MIND
by
Joseph Fram

WITH PEN IN HAND MY SWEET DOREEN
I'LL PAINT YOUR BEAUTY WITH A WORD
BUT MY PEN IS LOST INDEED
TO PAINT SUCH BEAUTY YET UNHEARD

FOR HOW WOULD ONE DESCRIBE A ROSE
TO THOSE WHO COULD NOT SEE OR TOUCH
OR WRITE OF COLORS FROM THE TREES
TO THINK YOU HAVE WOULD BE TOO MUCH

ALL THE WORDS I HAVE FOR YOU
CAN ONLY TELL YOU HOW I FEEL
ALL YOUR BEAUTY'S IN MY MIND
WORDS USED BEFORE SEEM SO UNREAL

HELP ME NOW MY SWEET DOREEN
COME TO MY MIND AND YOU WILL SEE
A PARADISE YOUR BEAUTY PAINTS
WHERE ONCE A DESERT USED TO BE

OH YES, I'LL KEEP MY PEN IN HAND
THE WORDS WILL COME I'M SURE, SOMEDAY
YOU CANNOT HIDE SUCH BEAUTY LONG
FOR WANT OF WORDS YOU CANNOT SAY

HEART WHOLE
by
Joseph Fram

I WAS BROKEN, DOWN AND OUT
DESPERATION FILLED MY SOUL
I KNEW MY LIFE WAS OVER
I WOULD NEVER BE HEART-WHOLE

MY FIRST LOVE, MY WIFE
MADE AWAY WITH SOMEONE NEW
AND I HAD OTHER BURDENS
I WAS TOLD I HAD CANCER TOO

I SLIPPED INTO DEPRESSION
KNEW NO ONE WANTED ME
I WAS JUST A SHELL THEN
THAT IS ALL THAT I WOULD BE

THEN SHE STEPPED INTO MY LIFE
SHE SAW ALL MY MEDS AND SUCH
TOOK ME GENTLY BY THE HAND
SHE DID NOT THINK IT WAS TOO MUCH

THAT VERY DAY CHANGED MY LIFE
I KNEW THAT GOD HAD HEARD MY CALL
MY BROKEN HEART BECAME A WHOLE
WHEN SHE ASKED ME "IS THAT ALL?"

IMPORTANT AT THAT TIME

by
Joseph Fram

AS I ADD CLOSURE TO MY LIFE
I LOOK BACK AT WHAT I'VE DONE
AGE HAS TEMPERED ALL MY DEEDS
KNOW NOT WHAT I'VE LOST OR WON

WHEN MY DEEDS WERE NEW BACK THEN
IN MY LIFE IT BROUGHT MUCH CHANGE
TURNING BACK THE PAGE OF TIME
PERHAPS OTHERS THOUGHT IT STRANGE

BUT THAT WAS THEN
'TWAS IN MY YOUTH
NO SHADES OF GRAY
AND ONLY TRUTH

BUT ALL THE DEEDS I DID BACK THEN
HAD SPECIAL VALUE JUST TO ME
SINCE IN MY MIND NO OTHERS DWELL
IT'S SOMETIMES HARD FOR THEM TO SEE

THEY WERE IMPORTANT AT THAT TIME
EACH DONE WITH CARE AND THOUGHT
VIEWING NOW THE PORTRAIT OF MY LIFE
WHICH PRECIOUS MEMORIES ARE FORGOT

ANOTHER POINT OF VIEW

by

Joseph Fram

I REALLY KINDA DIDN'T LIKE HIM
THOUGH HE WAS AN ORDINARY GUY
FOR ALL THE STUPID THINGS HE SAID
AND NEVER GAVE A THOUGHT A TRY

I KNEW IF I COULD CHANGE HIM
WE WOULD GET ALONG REAL WELL
BUT HE WOULD NEVER BEND MY WAY
NEVER WOULD, THAT, I COULD TELL

I WOULD PRESENT HIM WITH MY FACTS
HIS WOULD FOLLOW RIGHT BEHIND
WHEN I THOUGHT I HAD THE UPPER HAND
ANOTHER THOUGHT CAME FROM HIS MIND

IT MADE NO DIFFERENCE THAT WE TRIED
TO MAKE THE OTHER SEE OUR WAY
OUR MINDS WERE SET WITHIN OURSELVES
THAT IS HOW 'TWAS BOUND TO STAY

I THINK I GOT TO KINDA LIKE HIM
THOUGH THERE IS REALLY NOTHING NEW
I GUESS I JUST ACCEPT NOW
THAT HE HAS ANOTHER POINT OF VIEW

JAHLA

GRADUATION 2005
by
Joseph Fram

NOW THE TIME HAS FINALLY COME
YOUR HIGH SCHOOL GRADUATION DAY
YOU MADE ALL YOUR FAMILY PROUD
IN YOUR WORK AND SCHOOL AND PLAY

I KNOW AT TIMES YOU MIGHT HAVE SAID
I'D LIKE TO DO SOME OTHER THINGS
BUT IN THE END YOU STUCK IT OUT
FOR YOU KNOW WHAT GRADUATION BRINGS

HERE YOU ARE ALL GROWN AND FREE
AND SOON YOU WILL BE COLLEGE BOUND
ALL YOUR HIGH SCHOOL FUN AND MEMORIES
FOR ALL YOUR LIFE WILL BE AROUND

SO ENJOY EACH DAY IN FRONT OF YOU
AND KEEP YOUR FUTURE BRIGHT
ALWAYS STAY TRUE TO YOUR HEART
AND ALL WILL TURN OUT RIGHT

DON'T FORGET YOUR GRANDPA JOE
YOU KNOW HE LOVES YOU VERY MUCH
YOU WILL ALWAYS BE HIS JOLLYWAG
NO MATTER WHICH ROAD OF LIFE YOU TOUCH

CONGRATULATIONS
LOVE GRANDPA JOE

NEW YEAR BABY

by
Joseph Fram

HAPPY BIRTHDAY NEW YEAR BABY
YOU'VE TURNED INTO QUITE A LASS
YOU HAVE GROWN IN EVERY WAY
AND NOT ONCE HAVE LOST YOUR CLASS

WHEN YOU WERE BORN THAT DAY
YOUR MOTHER WAS PROUD AS CAN BE
LITTLE DID SHE KNOW BACK THEN
WHAT A GREAT PERSON TODAY WE'D SEE

YOU HAVE TAKEN ALL YOUR FAMILY
UNDER YOUR WING OF MOTHER HEN
FOR YOU HAVE ALWAYS BEEN SO CARING
IT ALL STARTED WAY BACK WHEN

ALL THE THINGS THAT YOU POSSESS
FROM LIFE'S LESSON YOU HAVE LEARNED
MOST OF WHICH YOU HAVE SHARED
AND ALL OF IT WELL EARNED

HAPPY BIRTHDAY TO YOU DENISE
MANY MORE FOR YOU TO GO
WITH THE BEST FROM ALL OF US
FOR YOU KNOW WE LOVE YOU SO

JUST A DRINK, PLEASE

by
Joseph Fram

I KNOW YOU MET THIS MAN BEFORE
THERE IS ONE IN EVERY CROWD
HE REALLY IS QUITE ANNOYING
THOUGH MOSTLY NOT TOO LOUD

HE DOES HAVE AN OPINION
ON EVERYTHING YOU SAY
IF YOU ARE DOING SOMETHING
HE'LL SHOW YOU ANOTHER WAY

WHEN HE ISN'T TALKING
HE STICKS HIS NOSE INTO A BOOK
IN CASE HE HAS MISSED SOMETHING
HE HAS TO TAKE ANOTHER LOOK

IT REALLY MAKES NO DIFFERENCE
THE SUBJECT MATTER NOW AT HAND
HE WILL GIVE YOU ALL THE DETAILS
TO TRY TO MAKE YOU UNDERSTAND

ALL THE THINGS INSIDE HIS HEAD
NO ONE CAN EVER TELL
WHY CAN'T HE POINT ME TO THE FOUNTAIN
NOT SHOW ME HOW TO DRILL A WELL

MY LITTLE DARLING
by
Joseph Fram

WELL MY LITTLE DARLING
THIS IS YOUR DAY OF SEVENTY-THREE
WE SPENT MANY YEARS APART
BUT NOW YOU ARE HERE WITH ME

THE TIME HAS JUST BEEN FLYING
YOU BRIGHTEN UP MY EVERY DAY
WHEN WE GET IN TROUBLE
YOU SEEM TO ALWAYS FIND THE WAY

DON'T YOU THINK IT IS REAL PRECIOUS
REMEMBERING THE WAY WE MET
AND ALL THE THINGS WE DO TOGETHER
IT WOULD BE SO HARD TO FORGET

NOW YOU TURN THE CORNER
OF A LIFE YOU BUILT SO FINE
AND ALL THE PARTS YOU PUT IN PLACE
I THANK YOU THAT YOU'RE MINE

HAPPY BIRTHDAY LITTLE DARLING
NEVER MIND OF ALL YOUR FEARS
FOR I'LL BE THERE TO LOVE YOU
TODAY AND THROUGHOUT THE YEARS

THE BATHROOM

by
Joseph Fram

WE HAVE A SECOND BATHROOM
THAT IS MOSTLY USED BY GUESTS
AND I HAVE NOTICED LATELY
SOME LEAVE THERE WITHOUT REST

SOME COME OUT SO DISGRUNTLED
THEY HARDLY SAY A WORD AT ALL
WHEN JUST BEFORE THEY WENT IN
THEY COULD TALK YOU UP A WALL

THEN OTHERS COME OUT SMILING
THEY ARE AS CHATTY AS CAN BE
THEY ARE FRIENDS WITH EVERYONE
AND EVEN GIVE A HUG TO ME

SO I BEGAN TO WONDER
WHAT DOES THE BATHROOM DO
TO CHANGE THE ONES THAT GO INSIDE
AND IT IS SO IMMEDIATE TOO

SO I STROLLED IN THE OTHER DAY
WHAT I WITNESSED MADE ME PALE
I NOW KNOW WHAT THE CULPRIT IS
IT IS OUR SECOND BATHROOM SCALE

NATTER

by
Joseph Fram

NATTER, NATTER, NATTER
SHE ALWAYS BUGS ME SO
ABOUT MY CLOTHES, THINGS I EAT
AND ALL THE PLACES THAT I GO

AS I START DOING SOMETHING
SHE HAS ONE TO TAKE ITS PLACE
TO DO HER CHORE I QUIT MINE
SO SHE HAS TWO JUST IN CASE

A SCENE I DO NOT WANT TO MAKE
SO WE CAN LIVE IN HARMONY
IF I COULD ONLY FIND THE WORDS
LIKE, YOU BE YOU AND I'LL BE ME

'TIS THEN I TAKE A LONELY STROLL
USE EVERY WORD THAT I CAN FIND
AND REALLY TELL HER WHAT I THINK
BUT I DO THIS ONLY IN MY MIND

THEN ONCE AGAIN I SEE HER
ALL IS AT PEACE INSIDE OF ME
FOR THERE IS NOTHING MORE TO SAY
I'VE SAID IT ALL BEFORE, YOU SEE

ODE TO CAROL

by
Joseph Fram

HAPPY BIRTHDAY CHRISTMAS CAROL
IT'S SO GOOD TO SEE YOU HERE
WITH ALL YOUR FRIENDS AND FAMILY
THAT HOLD YOU O' SO DEAR

CHRIST DID SUCH A CLEVER THING
TO HAVE YOU BORN ON CHRISTMAS DAY
IT IS SUCH A SPECIAL DAY FOR YOU
SINCE HE IS WITH YOU ALL THE WAY

NOW WE ARE NOT INTO ANY SECRETS
ABOUT WHAT ACTUAL AGE YOU ARE
ALL THE LOVE YOU HAVE SPREAD AROUND
EXCEEDS THOSE BIRTHDAY YEARS BY FAR

AS YOU WANDER THRU NEXT YEAR
I WISH A SMILE UPON YOUR FACE
IN KEEPING WITH YOUR SOUL INSIDE
FILLED WITH THE PRECIOUS GIFT OF GRACE

SO HAPPY BIRTHDAY TO YOU CAROL
MAY YOU HAVE MANY MORE
REMEMBER ALL THOSE THAT LOVE YOU
AND THOSE MEMORIES YOU CAN STORE

OURS

by

Joseph Fram

MY SEARCH IS OVER
I NO LONGER LOOK
IT IS CLEARLY WRITTEN
IN LIFE'S FICKLE BOOK

FOR LOVE HAS COME
IN A WAY UNKNOWN
TO HEARTS ONCE RESIGNED
TO STAY FOREVER ALONE

LOVE THAT CAN SEE
BEYOND HERE AND NOW
MADE FROM BROKEN PAST LOVES
MADE NOW MORE TENDER SOMEHOW

IN THIS LOVE WE HAVE FOUND
PEACE COMES TO THE HEART
WE ARE ALWAYS TOGETHER
THOUGH AT TIMES WE MUST PART

FOR SHE KNOWS THAT I WILL
AND I KNOW THAT SHE CAN
YOU SEE SHE'S MY WOMAN
AND I AM HER MAN

CHRISTMAS REMEMBERED

by
Joseph Fram

I WAS ASKING GOD
TO GIVE ME A REASON
WHY IN HIS NAME
WE CELEBRATE THIS SEASON

THE SEASON WAS CHOSEN
FOR THE DAY OF MY BIRTH
SO ALL WILL REMEMBER
WHY I CAME DOWN TO EARTH

NOW IF YOU RECALL
IT WAS PEACE FOR ALL MEN
AND I STILL HOPE AND PRAY
SOMEHOW WE DO IT AGAIN

ALL THE PRESENTS WE GIVE
AND SHARE WITH EACH OTHER
WILL MEAN SO MUCH MORE
IF WE LOVE ALL LIKE OUR BROTHER

SO PLEASE DON'T FORGET
MY MAIN MESSAGE IS LOVE
AND ALL YOU DO IN MY NAME
WILL BE BLESSED FROM ABOVE

OWN AGENDA
by
Joseph Fram

EACH HAS THEIR OWN AGENDA
WANT THINGS DONE THEIR WAY
TO THEM IT MAKES NO DIFFERENCE
WHETHER IT BE WORK OR PLAY

SOME LIKE TO TURN ATTENTION
ON A SPOTLIGHT THAT SAYS ME
WHILE OTHERS TRY TO SHARE
THE CREDIT FOR ALL TO SEE

WE HAVE A LITTLE PROCESS
THAT WE CALL COMPROMISE
WHEN WE SINCERELY USE IT
IT MAKES ALL SEEM SO WISE

WHEN ALL IS SAID AND DONE
MOST TIMES IT MATTERS NOT A WIT
AND IT QUICKLY LEAVES OUR MIND
IF WE THINK AT ALL OF IT

BUT WE ALL HAVE OUR OWN AGENDA
NO MATTER HOW CLOSELY WE AGREE
IF THEY HAD TAKEN MY DESIGN
OH, HOW MUCH BETTER IT WOULD BE

SALUTE TO DELLA

by
Joseph Fram

WE SALUTE YOU OUR DEAR DELLA
NOW WE CELEBRATE YOUR LIFE
AS A FRIEND, SISTER, SCHOLAR, SAILOR
MOTHER, GRANDMOTHER AND A WIFE

WE REMEMBER THAT YOU ENTERED
THE BIG WAR IN NINETEEN FORTY-TWO
WHILE OTHERS STAYED AT HOME
YOUR PATRIOTIC DUTY YOU MUST DO

AFTER HELPING BRING PEACE TO EARTH
A WIFE AND MOTHER YOU BECAME
IN FREEDOM YOU RAISED YOUR FAMILY
THEY'VE BROUGHT HONOR TO YOUR NAME

WHEN YOU KNEW 'TWAS TIME TO GO
THE PEACE OF GOD IS WHAT YOU FOUND
WITH YOUR FAMILY AND THEIR OFFSPRING
YOUR FINAL MOMENTS TO SURROUND

NOW A FLAG WILL DRAPE YOUR COFFIN
AND ETERNAL REST YOU WILL FIND
BUT WITH US YOU WILL LIVE FOREVER
WE WILL KEEP YOU IN OUR MIND

PEN TO PAPER

by

Joseph Fram

WHEN I PUT PEN TO PAPER
MY MIND SOMETIMES DRAWS A BLANK
I IMAGINE IN ITS RECESSES
BLIND ALLEYS DARK AND DANK

BUT WHEN I AM ASKED TO SPEAK
I COULD TALK FOR DAYS AND DAYS
ABOUT THE THINGS I'VE DONE AND DO
IN A THOUSAND DIFFERENT WAYS

SPEAKING COMES QUITE EASILY
SOMETIMES I WILL INVENT A WORD
SOME PEOPLE THAT MAY LISTEN
WISH IT WAS ONE THEY NEVER HEARD

PUTTING PEN TO PAPER
IS NOT SUCH AN EASY TASK
IN MY BRAIN THERE IS A CRAMP
THAT WAS THERE BEFORE YOU ASK

SO I STUMBLE AND I FUMBLE
TO WRITE THE WORDS I WANT TO SAY
THEN WHAT WILL ALWAYS CROSS MY MIND
IS WILL THEY READ THEM ANYWAY

PRAYER IN POETRY
by
Joseph Fram

LORD I BELIEVE YOU ARE HERE
YOU LIVE IN MY SOUL AND HEART
THOUGH OTHERS TRY TO TURN ME
THEY CANNOT KEEP US APART

I HAVE LOOKED INTO RELIGION
EACH SAYS THEY ARE THE ONE
BUT IN THE END THEY ARE THE SAME
THEY ALL ASK "THY WILL BE DONE"

I FIND IT HARD TO FATHOM
YOU CHOOSE ONE OVER THE OTHER
FOR NO MATTER HOW WE LOOK OR SPEAK
UNDER OUR SKIN LIVE SISTER AND BROTHER

THE GOD THAT LIVES INSIDE OF ME
IS MADE OF PEACE AND GENTLE CHARM
THERE IS NO PLACE FOR WAR AND DEATH
HE TRIES TO KEEP US FROM ALL HARM

IF I AM WRONG IN MY BELIEF
I COME WITH AN OPEN HEART
IF I FAIL IN ANY WAY
I DO THE BEST TO FILL MY PART

RESURRECTION

by
Joseph Fram

FOR EACH THERE IS A SHINING STAR
ON THE DAY THAT WE ARE BORN
THE JOURNEY THROUGH OUR LIFE
BEGINS THAT VERY MORN

FOR EACH THERE IS A TEMPLE
WHERE WE LEARN WRONG FROM RIGHT
TO TEACH US ALL THE VALUES
FOR WHICH WE STAND AND FIGHT

EACH WILL HAVE OUR MAGDELINE
WHO WILL LOVE US COME WHAT MAY
FOR IN HER EYES WE ARE A KING
NO MATTER WHAT THE WORLD WILL SAY

THEN THERE IS OUR CROSS TO BEAR
EVEN WHEN ALL KNOW IT IS WRONG
BUT WE WILL HAVE OUR SIMON
SO WE DON'T CARRY IT TOO LONG

AND DEATH WILL FOLLOW HEARTBREAK
SEND US INTO THE DEPTHS OF HELL
THROUGH DEATH COMES RESURRECTION
THAT MAKES US WHOLE AND WELL

REUNION

by

Joseph Fram

I WENT TO MY CLASS REUNION
FROM A CLASS SO LONG AGO
I HAD VISIONS IN MY MIND
OF CLASSMATES I USED TO KNOW

WHEN I GOT TO MY HOMETOWN
TO ME IT APPEARED SO STRANGE
I SUPPOSE I EXPECTED GROWTH
BUT NOT REALLY THIS MUCH CHANGE

OH, THE SCHOOL WAS STILL STANDING
AND THE PLAYGROUND WAS THE SAME
BUT THERE WAS A FUNNY SIGN OUTSIDE
WITH A RATHER FOREIGN NAME

GONE WERE THE NUNS HERDING CHILDREN
THE LAUGHTER AT RECESS I WOULD HEAR
THE BELLS TO END OUR JOYFUL PLAYTIME
ALL THE MEMORIES I HOLD DEAR

I LEFT THAT REUNION EMPTY
IT'S NOT FOR ME THAT I FEEL SAD
IT IS ALL THE CHILDREN THERE NOW
WILL MISS THE GOOD TIMES THAT I HAD

SHARE

by
Joseph Fram

WE SAID WE'D SHARE
ALL THE THINGS WE HAD
WE'D SHARE THE GOOD
AND SHARE THE BAD

WE'D SHARE OUR YOUTH
TILL WE GOT OLD
WE'D SHARE ALL THINGS
BUT WHY A COLD

SOMETIMES

by
Joseph Fram

SOMETIMES WHEN WE WAKE UP
EVERYTHING WE DO IS WRONG
WE TRY BUT WE CAN'T FIX IT
IT CONTINUES ALL DAY LONG

SOMETIMES WE ARE CHARMED
EVERYTHING WE DO IS RIGHT
ALL THE PIECES FALL INTO PLACE
FROM DAWN TILL DARK OF NIGHT

MOSTLY THINGS STAY EVEN
THEY ARE THE SAME EACH DAY
THIS HELPS US GET THROUGH LIFE
WHICH SEEMS TO BE THE BETTER WAY

WHEN YOU MEASURE UPS AND DOWNS
THEY EVEN OUT MORE OR LESS
WHICH CYCLE WE REMEMBER
IS LEFT TO EACH ONE'S GUESS

SOMETIMES WE ARE SUCCESSFUL
SOMETIMES WE ARE DOOMED TO FAIL
SOMETIMES WE ARE THE HAMMER
AND SOMETIMES WE ARE THE NAIL

SOUL MATES

by

Joseph Fram

IF YOU BELIEVE IN SOUL MATES
YOU LIVE A VERY SPECIAL LIFE
FOR YOUR PEACE IS ENDLESS
VIRTUALLY FREE OF STRIFE

FOR IT IS SAID THAT SOUL MATES
COME FROM A DIFFERENT TIME AND PLACE
IF THEY DO NOT CONNECT IN THIS LIFE
IN A FUTURE ONE THEY WILL EMBRACE

THEY HAVE MET IN A LIFE BEFORE
BUT THEIR LOVE WAS TORN APART
AND THEIR SOULS SEEK EACH OTHER
UNTIL THEY CAN MEND THAT BROKEN HEART

ALL THE WHILE THEY ARE APART
THEY KNOW THEY WILL MEET ONCE MORE
THERE IS A PEACE INSIDE THEIR SOULS
THEY WILL BE HAPPY AS BEFORE

ONCE SOUL MATES ARE PUT IN PLACE
THEIR SPIRIT JOURNEY ENDS
THEY WILL BE FOREVERMORE
HAPPY LOVERS, MATES AND FRIENDS

THANK YOU SCOTLAND

by
Joseph Fram

SURELY SCOTLAND HATED MANKIND
AND IT HAPPENED LONG AGO
THEY HAVE MADE EVERY NATION SUFFER
IT MAKES NO DIFFERENCE WHERE YOU GO

THEY WENT AND MADE THEIR BAGPIPES
A JOKE 'TWAS MEANT TO BE
BUT WHEN IT SCARED THE MICE AWAY
THEY HELD ON TO THEM YOU SEE

THEN LOOK AT THE DRINK THEY MADE
A SCOTCH TO BURN YOU UP INSIDE
IT TAKES YOUR MIND AND MAKES YOU DUMB
AND WOBBLY LEGS THAT YOU CAN'T HIDE

THEN REVENGE ON MANKIND CAME
THE GAME OF GOLF, THEIR LASTING CURSE
FOR EVERYONE THAT PLAYS THE GAME
THE MORE YOU PLAY, THE MORE YOU'RE WORSE

SO HOW CAN THEY NOT HATE MANKIND
THE BAGPIPES PIERCE YOUR EAR
THEIR WHISKEY TASTES LIKE FIRE
THEY MADE A HOLE YOU CAN'T GET NEAR

A FATHER'S LOVE
by
Joseph Fram

IF I DIDN'T TELL YOU
THERE WOULD BE A SADNESS INSIDE ME
YOU ARE MY ONLY DAUGHTER
AND ALWAYS YOU WILL BE

BUT NOW YOU TAKE A DIFFERENT TURN
A FATHER HAS TO SPEAK HIS MIND
THOUGH I CANNOT LIVE YOUR LIFE
PEACE AND LOVE I HOPE YOU'LL FIND

THERE IS A BEAUTY IN YOUR HEART
WITH ALL YOU WANT TO SHARE
IF I DON'T TELL YOU HOW I FEEL
THEN SURELY IT'S THAT I DON'T CARE

THE MAN TO WHOM YOU GIVE YOURSELF
HAS CHILDREN SCATTERED ALL AROUND
AND SEVERAL WIVES BEFORE YOUR TIME
WILL THERE BE MORE THAT CAN BE FOUND?

NOW HE'S AS FREE AS HE CAN BE
HIS CHILDREN LEFT WITH MANY WIVES
I CANNOT HELP BUT WONDER NOW
HOW THAT WILL AFFECT INTO YOUR LIVES

THE OBVIOUS
by
Joseph Fram

WHEN WE OVERLOOK THE OBVIOUS
WE ARE SOMETIMES TOO INTENSE
WE FIX DON'T NEED FIXING THINGS
THAT REALLY DOESN'T MAKE MUCH SENSE

I RECALL AN ELECTRICAL PROBLEM
TO REPAIR WE DUG A DITCH
WHEN SUDDENLY THE LIGHTS WENT ON
SOMEONE THOUGHT TO THROW THE SWITCH

THEN THE TIME I SPENT HOURS
FILLING OUT SOME STORE REBATE
THEN I NOTICED AT THE BOTTOM
I SURPASSED THE EXPIRATION DATE

SOME ASSEMBLY MAY BE REQUIRED
QUICKLY BRINGS ME TO MY KNEES
I MUST OVERLOOK THE OBVIOUS
WHEN I WORK THEIR A'S AND B'S

AFTER YEARS OF MISPLACED EFFORT
I CAREFULLY READ EACH LITTLE THING
BUT I MUST OVERLOOK THE OBVIOUS
WITH EACH NEW FAILURE THAT THEY BRING

THIS MAN

by
Joseph Fram

WHAT IS IT WORTH TO KNOW THIS MAN
IT SURELY CROSSED HER MIND
WILL HE BE LIKE ALL THE REST
OR IS HE A TREASURE THAT I FIND

ALL IN THE PAST DID VENT THEIR IRE
WHEN SOMETHING DID GO WRONG
THAT'S WHEN THE TIES OF LOVE UNWRAPPED
THE END DID NOT TAKE TOO LONG

BUT WHEN WE ERRED, HE SMILED AT ME
NOTHING'S BAD AS IT FIRST SEEMS
WE MUST BE TENDER AT THESE TIMES
LEST WE SHATTER ALL OUR DREAMS

STILL I LOOK TO TOUCH THIS MAN
THE LOVE HE HAS MUST BE FOR REAL
THERE IS NO WAY HE COULD BE SO WARM
IF DEEP INSIDE THAT'S NOT HIS FEEL

PERHAPS AT LAST I FOUND SOMEONE
THAT WILL CAREFULLY GUARD MY HEART
FOR IF HE IS THE MAN I THINK
I DEEM THAT WE SHOULD NEVER PART

Books by Joseph Fram:

Joseph's Journey, Volume 1
Poetry of Hope, Help, Healing and Humor

Joseph's Journey, Volume 2
Psychological Concepts Expressed in Poetry

Joseph's Journey, Volume 3
A Look at the Flip Side of My Life

‒ ‒ ‒ ‒ ‒ ‒ ‒ ‒ ‒ ‒ ‒ ‒

Coming soon!
Joseph's Journey, Volume 4

Take the next step
with Joseph in the journey of a
lifetime.

Everlasting Publishing
P.O. Box 1061
Yakima, WA 98907

www.ingramcontent.com/pod-product-compliance
Lightning Source LLC
Chambersburg PA
CBHW021145020426
42331CB00005B/908